CYPRESS

CYPRESS
Barbara Klar

for Patrick, (Lane)
with thanks, admiration,
and all best wishes.

Barbara Klar

Saskatoon

January 2011

Brick Books

Library and Archives Canada Cataloguing in Publication

Klar, Barbara, 1966-
    Cypress / Barbara Klar.

Poems.
ISBN 978-1-894078-67-2

I. Title.

PS8571.L367C96 2008   C811'.54   C2008-903162-8

We acknowledge the Canada Council for the Arts, the Government
of Canada through the Book Publishing Industry Development
Program (BPIDP), the Saskatchewan Arts Board and the Ontario
Arts Council for their support of our publishing program.

Cover photograph, "Chrysalis," 2006, by Barbara Klar.
Author photograph by Julia MacRae.

The book is set in Sabon.

Design and layout by Alan Siu.

Printed and bound by Sunville Printco Inc.

Brick Books
431 Boler Road, Box 20081
London, Ontario N6K 4G6

www.brickbooks.ca

for the spirit of Uisge Beatha, a deerhound

I call out to the stone,
and the stone
calls back

    – Galway Kinnell

CONTENTS

WINDLIGHT

Forward

Opposite north. Almost Montana. I am a tree planter
climbing switchbacks to the last contract of spring: first
gear, horizon tilting, parallel again. The dirt road crosses
a grass plateau fluted by the trees of the Cypress Hills, the
corner no one ever goes to, deep in elk and lodgepole pine,
deep in the land of the dead. A sorrow enters my breathing,
a spore for this anomalous place above the prairie, the
highest land between the Rockies and Labrador, an island
of altitude, a country the glaciers flowed around instead
of over. These were the strange hills of vision quests, the
last hunting grounds of the starving. Twenty Assiniboine
murdered by wolfers over some missing horses, and the
Mounties marched west, bringing order, order.

The crew walks to work through June rains that vaguely
remember humans. Things grow here that shouldn't:
mountain flowers, pines that need fire to regenerate, the
lodgepoles the Métis named *cyprès*, their cones last opened
in the great flames of 1886. Now there are no fires. The
oldest stands are cut blocks. I am a body heeling seedlings
into the stones, *les montagnes des cyprès* mistranslating to
the Cypress Hills, a place some of the locals call Cypress.

I go back and I go back, autumns after summers, a hundred
walks arcing. I walk up and down, planting nothing. I lie in
my tent at night, listening for ghosts. What little they say I
write down.

PLANTER

Conglomerate Cliff Road, Approach

Cobblestone, washboard, a bicycle getting nowhere
but rattled, the poem not a ride but a walk
through fescue and stones. I lay down
my sorry implement. Wind arrives
inside me. Boots draw a crooked line,
connect the stones, draw a picture of the way,
a line shadow swirls in like water, crushed grass
beginning to forget me. Through the land without
cliffs I carry water to the start of my vanishing,
the cliffs wait for me, the way home
will weigh nothing but peace.

Somewhere in the forest a cookstove door
rusts into the underworld, a ring beside
the Cozy-Glo remembers a hand. The wind
holds stones together but it blew away
the rancher and his wife in 1951: a pool
of snowmelt used to last them all summer,
her only mirror, that little lake, and the vista
from the cliffs, her face shining back from the glass
of the Great Sand Hills a hundred miles in the distance.

How long have I been walking, four hours,
four years? I will see to the edge of the world
but not the future. In the high blur, *Pinus contorta*,
what must be the cliffs: sky drops through
the stomach of its blue. I drink
my last water. I will see beyond wind.
My boots run a line through grass, a creek
of shadow, when I turn its dark light
falls past my feet and I arrive.

Talk

I came as a planter to the Cypress Hills and my father came as a soldier to the Carpathian Mountains. He was on his way to the war, he wasn't there yet, and I had arrived at the shovels against the stones, the slash wound bleeding into the rock wound into the mind. I took the seedlings into the ruined cities and the west rolled over in its sleep, the wars inside the earth making mountains. I planted trees around the cattle in the soft, low mountains and I did not sleep among the steaming cattle, my hand opened the mountains and I did not march over and through them, I parted the earth, its stone fish, and I did not ask the shrapnel on the other side what it would feel like, a metal fish knocking bone, a star and blood's tail, a burning needle. Ernie from Ruddelle once asked *Does your hound know what a porcupine is?* and I said *No, and I hope she never learns,* and the mind flowed into the arrow of her face and the quills sewing night into a demon, her one velvet arrow and the army that lets her live. I came as a planter to the two thousand houses I dug into the stones every day, and my father is marching the last blue mountain sixty years after his mountains. Sometimes you have to march. The world has gone crazy since the golden fear of its childhood, and the deer that isn't deer is darker willow, and the deer holds up its question, *death or listen?* and talk, talk is weight. The hound with her fine limp marches with me, our steps the only sound. Deer cross the forests and wait for one another and my blood is very old, a river in a valley, a sound.

Ranger Station Road

I walk down into the valley where I was last
young, down into the darkness of the wisdom
of alder, down into willow's old need
for water, down to the winding world,
the trout-jumping valley of flowers
and money and love

                and the only barnyard
for days of walking, a bluebird warbling
truly on the only sign since Maple Creek:
West Block Ranger Station, established 1917,
the flag of the Dominion
come before me,

             I am walking down a rutted
road two horses wide into having been
a tree planter, twenty-seven and immortal
in the valley of the never dead, the ghosts
of all the rangers riding.

                 Somewhere in the hills
the invisible part cowboy part cop
is protecting me. I'll only see him
if I'm lost and he must find
me, if someone's death is lost
and he must find me.

              My shovel leg
is aching. My dog and my truck and my father
are all on borrowed time. Wooden bridges grieve

the downward sleep of the green blood of water,
nothing waiting but the black friends
of my fears in the valley where the dead
will watch for me,

                the grizzlies
and the invisible gazing from
their vision posts, everything alone
with itself. I wait for the horseman
to take off his hat and call me ma'am,
his words falling down
to the valley.

Gravity, The First Tower Road

I am born into the sound for hills,
the weighted singing. The bird
was my mother, her feathers are stone
and bones are hollow rattles. The bird
was my father, soon he will be flying
up the steep road that leads to a tower.
I climb, mostly lung, breathing and breathing
our song of constant air. I am the bird who walks
on feathers, early animal, syllable, seed
of the strong race of deer. When I fly
it is a running, the wings of grass a family
for my hooves. My song is not a sigh
but a remembering: left, my heavy wing
before the right one, the sun pressing blood
from the grasses. I walk and walk until
tomorrow and tomorrow. I curl
at the feet of pines.
I wait.

Storm

My mouth is a ball of lightning remembering
streets. Deer smell the cities, the fear of deer.
Between their nostrils and my mouth are the streaming
invisible pages of *A Field Guide to Growing Old*
and *The Introduction to Questions*, green airs
saying only *welcome.*

The mouth is an empty ear.

The eye is a lost moon wobbling above the planet Grass.

The heart is a stone flipped over by the brave frosts.

The spine is a lodgepole apprentice.

And the mouth, the end of fire, listens forward to the wind.

Work Road, North Benson Trail

In the workless Cypress Hills the trees are feathers pointing cloudward and the green angels sing me down. Five years after, I walk this road in mercy's direction, down, south, down, the weightless autumn carrying me, the evening carrying the sandwiches and apples in my belly, the rain and snow in my skin, the endorphin resolutions in my hard blue lungs. That was the contract of cobblestone and broken shovel until the white rains parted the stones to an easy $300 a day, and the morning road north was too slick for anything to haul us. We had to walk. Rock-slow and stubborn, we pressed toward the summit of North Benson Trail, sweet arrival dangling from the clouds and pulling upward, always one more guise of the vertical in the three mile hypotenuse, old Benson in the mountain fog, laughing. All of the others passed through my breath: hunter with my arrows on my back, gatherer, my babies following, logger with my saws and horses, my quadriceps burning, first planter, last planter, seedlings pointed at the ancient pines and the spaces I filled between them. Two thousand times a day I bent over, and I would bend for two thousand days to walk down North Benson Trail. Five years after my last tree, south still leads to bed and all hills are possible, the gravities carrying me down by the fronts of the ankles. At my back the little lodgepoles are holding up the heady air. At my back a muddy ribbon flutters up the mountain and in my body the hills float down.

Name

The land is broken in three, a spine buckling
the horizon. *Broken Back. Three Backs.*
I am the old woman drawn up and down,
my body absorbing silence, my body
sweating noise. The No Longer Needed
drips to the stones whose blessings
stare and say nothing. Where the land
gets broken I am broken, bones
sticking out of me, content in their pieces,
marrow noises falling. I grow the scar
of glaciers, the name carved smooth:
The Place Where the Land Gets Broken.

West, the ice answers. East.
In between, a crossing.

Clear-Cut, North Plateau

I must go there, to the clear-cut
of my madness, to the saw light, the bone ground,

the battlefield smouldering with absence. Sky falls
on the fallen, three poplars stand like the last men

whistling their names. A skidder track
opens before me, grass clamped onto its job

in the new world of scars, sky landing
its noisy light on the targets of the growth rings.

My sorrows fall, the cities unfallen, the towers rising
far away. I am forest running from my families,

the woodcutter avoiding the stare of stones
and the seep of acidity, kinnickinnick

seeking the vertical. I am the fearer of pines
crossing deserts of their ashes, my hands

over my ears, light crushing through the stumps
big as turbines. The forest was darkness

because I was darkness. The ghost of the forest
is noise because I am the machine.

Insomnia, Fear of Rain

In the high sleep, half sleep, unfinished business
booms in the west like the speed of blue horses
faster than running, forests knock me down.
I fear the gods, their rain drowning air,
the liquid flesh of thunder in the dirt road
out, impassible, impossible. When it rains
in the Cypress Hills there is no leaving,
dawn to its axles in mud, hills circling
like a posse of silence. I will fight them.
My fear of heights and death and dentists
and mistakes and love and water
will fight them, my fallen fears,
their black cones flowering the bone
across my chest with the fear
of never being found, the fear
of hills forever, the fear
in my throat:
wing.

The End of Squares

Curves are imperfect.
Vistas roll out of the mist.
In the dark schools of the hills
blood remembers dry arithmetic,
the square names of fields.

Blood crashes along, miscalculating deadfall.
There is more than one answer here
and there is no question. The fallen
point their spears at my fall.
I am impaled by lodgepole, arrow
of the poison hills, old blood rushing
from sternum to heart.

Now that I am pine all the arrows
leap before me. Hills are the only home.
My scab is bark, an emblem. My scar
grows twin green hairs.

Nine Inches of Rain

No radio contact, a valley so deep the signals can't find it. And so I write from the grey hills far into the rain to a lover who loved stone, the spear and the hand and the rain parting stone, our room bright and granite, rolling forward.

In the valley of missing I write toward stone from the third night of weather. The tent walls weep, sleeping bag a misery-fuse wicking up rain and my hands will not stop drowning, they hold the rippled paper like a white raft, they pray for a messenger, a rock slide, wind, a bottle crossing water. *You are the rain's opposite,* I write, *you are a bone of fire.* The creek swells to my damp, drumming sleeplessness, and the creek that will not stop rising is lonely also, thinking Milk River, Missouri, Mississippi, Atlantic, nothing left to enter but the salt dream of its winding.

Valley so deep the oceans have forgotten it, sky wringing dry. I can smell the stone. It is rolling full of missing in a steaming line between the sun and someone who thinks of me. It is the bright vessel. It is the land I wait for.

South Benson Trail, The Stone Road

To walk uphill keep your eyes on the ground.
Stones distract from the work of climbing, show you
their pace, the lung wish, the getting there
not winded.

You must take home one stone.
Stop looking for the stone.
When it sees you coming it will be seen.

Stones move through your lungs
and your eyes, in their climbing, become lungs.
Feet, legs, arms, mouth, eyes become lungs. Air,
not muscle, ascends you. Look back at the distance.
Air has brought you higher and stones,
the opposite of air, have shown you the way.

Stones take on the nature of those who bring them
home. Because life was heavy the stones
on your windowsills became dark and heavy,
more possessions every time you moved, junk
to block the light. You drove to the country in the middle
of the summer night and let them go. In the life
without stones your darkness was clumsy, your muscles
were idle, your eyes were blinded by the lack
of silhouettes. You *want* a life with weight.

You allow yourself one stone. When it sees
you coming it will be seen, heavy in its onlyness.

Stones are the vertebrae of hills,
ripe apples, brains packed with
truth, pages scraped with the alphabet of glaciers,
stones are eyes with moss lids, faceless clocks, coins
in the ancient currency, stones are plates steaming
with their meals of light, are light bulbs, the hail
of brainstorms, stones will warm your bed, testicles
wanting, teeth grinding, pencil leads grinding,
stones are the nerves of sand, electric,
and stones, in their silence,
mark the dead.

And so you stop looking for the stone,
will not choose but be chosen, caught by the line
of the stone's sight, blinked at by the southwest
light where evening begins. *Here.*
You are chosen. By a palm-sized, ellipsoidal,
large small potato stone, yellow and scraped
with a brown *K*, dented spine. *X* marks
the stone, begins the story, stone full
of sun in your right hand listening,
egg in the pocket.

When you leave it will choose
its place against light, a song in your empty house
but for now keep climbing or not. Full of stones,
your lungs breathe the million-year-old air.

Cumulus, Vertigo

Above all my leavings
I am incapable of love.
Forget, say the dead who named
the Beautiful Highlands, Sweet Pine Mountains,
                                        Thunder Breeding Hills.

In the meadows bruised by snow
the shooting stars have landed,
their distant pasts flaming.

Rain rises. The sea is only
rumour and the future is wind.

The dead have waited in their robes,
the anthered dead, the purple animals
naming my grave.

FIRE

Sap's Song

Pine blood, sweetness, long light, river,
golden upward blood from the wound
of equinox, I sing the pitch of waking.
Darkness breathes, darkness
breathes the start of fever
in the belly of the cold lung
hungering light. I am pine bark's
downward traveller, resin berry,
April bitter of the hills singing Taste This:
spring addicts the winter, cures the throat,
the tuberculoses, the ancient rotting scurvies.
I seal the vessel of walking, I rub
myself on the paths, poultice
for the fevered in the rising
forest, in the swirling forest.

East Tower Trail, The Bone

Early May. I walk through fescue's heat,
the plateau greening. They have been through
winter since I was last here, the hills made
of the parting ice. In a crease of the hills
I find the bone of a snowdrift and lie
in it, the bed remembering the northwest wind
falling here, here, here, five, fifteen feet of snow,
I am losing my way, grains of snow cutting
my face shoving forward in a former life,
white man trapper up Shit Creek.

Today I will not die. I walk toward summer
with a snowball in my left hand, white candy-apple
from the children of the hills, wise and bitten
by the cold. I eat the letting go of snow,
a saving of snow until hills can be hills
without it. They don't care that I returned.
They are busy loving time. I walk across
their task, the winter of the grass
giving way, the way I follow.

The Blessing

I check the hound for ticks, brush its fur
backward and the hound leans into
my bristled hand. I part the fur on its rump
to the white underwool, my eye worrying
arachnids shiny as dimes, my mother eye
believing Lyme disease, tick paralysis,
Rocky Mountain spotted fever. The hound
leans and grins. Let it think brushing is praise
for the blind love walking just ahead of me
to the ends of hills, its nostrils blessing
the willow wolves, foot pads answering
the muddy valentines left in the night
by deer.

     June has loosened
hound fur. I clean the brush and throw
the soft fistful to the creek, a wren nest
floating, paper boat bobbing over rocks
and logs and out of sight. I brush the guard hairs
of the topline, the brindle ribs of the chest, the black-tipped
deer fur of the withers. Brush after brushful is taken
by water like clumps of cumulocirrus, old women's
heads drifting into polar bears, little deaths turning
toward the river and hills
across the sea.

     All day the hound
has walked just ahead of me. All night
the beat of its sleep will fill our chests,
fire hound in my sleeping bag, bone hound
on *The Book of Nightmares*, a goose stretched

over the moving egg of dream. Winter sheds
from its follicles. I check the hound for ticks,
its feet for cactus spines, its chest
for spears:

　　　　　now we may sleep
and tomorrow the hound will bless my way,
the hound who shakes its dust away like a hound
who has walked out of water, the hound
whose boat has arrived.

The Fire Branch

I come to the tree. This
is a lodgepole to be buried beneath, hair roots
worming through vertebrae, taproot cracking pelvis,
femurs turning to the dream of root, the tree
my rotting's
stone.

I bury an orange peel in the needles beside
a grounded branch: lost limb, fallen antler,
fine log of driftwood, fuel for my fire. These
are things it resembles. I must pick one,
name what I take. Never warmed by lodgepole,
I name the branch *cremation* and grass
releases it. We walk,

             my torso angled
like an arrow to the wind, my right arm
cradling the wide end to my hip, other end
dragging over stones, one twig and a cone
sticking skyward,

           to my camp,
over the beaver dams, through the willow
jungles, across the happy meadows of arnica.
The branch follows. It trusts. It snags on nothing,
comes along like a pack horse loving its load,
the anti-load coming with me.

Having given wind its skin
a branch gives bone to fire
and its ash
to night.

I pour a cup of wine
and with my swede saw, rest,
ponder the aesthetics of woodpiles:

a dozen sticks, cone
still skewed, antenna
into the dusk,

a stack of grey arms,

and the shoulder, its own pile,
defier of the saw—the splinter
was the cleaving point when lightning struck,
wrong place at the time, sap spurting red
as thunder—a hump that waits to burn
in one piece and completely.

Let the dark bless the branch and the wine
my blood. I have worked and it is cold
now, the match's shiver answered
by paper.

Deep in the lodgepole night
I am poured into fire.
Log after next-sized log
fire knows what it saw:
ash,
no men,
grass,
the first man,
many seedlings,
elk grazing by,
geese barking south,
drifting snow,
fifty winters,
wolf on the move,
forty springs,
ice to water,
green clouds,
thunder,
axes.

My last log is lightning
igniting the oldest heat.
Lodgepole, lodgepole, windwood bone
from the twisted tree that will be my stone,
arm from the tree that will hold my bones:
burn for the night, burn for the night.

Gap Road, The Last White Spruce

Low grass after the wildflowers, low
as ocean long after water. Earth is dry.
Skeletons rise. Pine surrenders, spruce surrenders,
poplar surrenders to the grass and I am naked,
the green cloaks behind me, the road streaming
through the deep hills, the sky following the red weed
of my skin, sky of the hammer-blue eye
and the wind between two forests.

Seán is meeting me at four o'clock on the other side
of the Gap. I must march so the sky
cannot eat more of me, blue monster making
weather of my hair and blood
by the start of the afternoon.
Cold with hurry I must march through
the terror of the grass's liquid waves.
I march toward the pine wall of the castle
of hope. I hold onto solids, non-winds:
a truck's piece of chrome, an evicted stone
and a cow's lumbar vertebra, the seventh angel
of drought, her calcium wings fallen
from the water of bovine flesh.

The sky is monster because
space is the mirror of those who fear

and the boa root of the last
white spruce holds onto its coulee, the last
until the end of Gap Road. This is how
I rest, once, with the spine bone of a cow
who died of space below the tree
that grows from less, the bone bleached
ivory by the sky's disease: the coyotes
shattered out of it and ran her down.
She is the hard bird entering my hand
between the third and fourth metacarpi,
flying my arm to the pumping rib to graze
the blood inside me. She is the angel

of why I walk the Gap. Long ago
when I had hooves my hunger passed
between two forests. There would be
the sweet flowers, the needles of pine
and grass on the other side. I fell and the sun
ate my waters. When the rains finally came
they drove me deep into the earth and I grazed
below the great gaps for two hundred droughts
and the sky with its dry mouth pulls me out
at last, my bone that smells
of time, my wingstone
on its way to the other side.

West Tower Trail, Fear of Hills

You are lost,
have lost everything about you
except sadness and the direction
home is. You say your name
to the sun and the sun has you
repeat yourself, your body
without features
doing everything you do
against the grass. Keep to the right
of this shadow. You will be walking
southeast through trees that all look the same
through a pasture of strangeness to a valley
you've slept in many nights, a rudimentary bed
with a hill's arm around you, a thing to cook on, a radio.
This is the way: fear of the hills inside you. You followed
a map and some orange paint on trees, climbed
over deadfall at Benson Creek, changed
direction with every step to cross it and now
you are lost, trusting the sun
that repeats your shape to the left
of your path. You are lost in another
way. You want to lie down tonight with a map
of sadness. Even in their folding
the hills lead you to you.

Tower Road

I have watched the tower from across
the valley. I have watched a road, no, pieces
of road, threads falling north from the cloth of roads,
a lost road asking the reasons for roads, road

across three miles of sky, cloud road,
cirrus white, road crawling from forests
and crossing grass, snake road, winder,
diamonded with cobblestone, man road

carved by machine, gouge on the face
of the north slope, beauty line in the light
that knows the way, yellow brick stairway
into evening, heaven, the road on no map.

Where it leads I have not asked. It climbs.

Walking falls into my body and lands
in the pieces of time: a ladder, smoke, binoculars,
a towerman's summers just above the forest, the road
no longer a question but two clay tracks forgetting tires,
loving grass's adamance and the relic of the DNR.
I climb the south-facing hills on the road
of here and now, of autumn worship, of bowing head
and clasping hands at the bottom of my spine,
road of my fathers through black woods, of the steady air
entering and emptying my lungs, road of the bending road,
the mind turning back on itself, legs remembering
being half as old, forests, they all led here,
I remember walking to a tower
with my mother and father when even they
were young, the poplars burning off
their summers in the blue afternoon, no need
to speak. The rock road steepened,
the tower sudden, hovering above the trees,
no Babylon, no Pisa but an orange cupola
on a tree of steel, a compass needle pointing
at itself, a windowed hexagon mirroring the sky
and the falling fire of leaves. I never thought
it would be so beautiful. The day burned
into me, into my legs that could have walked
further, into my lungs that would remember
the fire-coloured air.

Old age topples to the grey horizontals,
no young trees. A hundred and twenty years
since a fire freed the seeds from their patient
resined cones. Into the lodgepoles
yearning for fire: I am the youngest
thing here, my ignorance of ashes
climbing Tower Road toward the only
human sign in the dreaming Crown-owned pines:
their eight-walled plywood keeper, landmark
for the lost, hawk perch over weasel fire,
lighthouse for the stones rolling
forward through a hundred and twenty memories
of fire, the stones who split in sleep and wake
with the smoking wisdom of the burned.
I come to the tower at the top of the hills
and the forest must be lost
to begin itself again. The fire will come
at night, golden cloaks roaring, the ravens
will fly at the sky's white heat and go
with fire to the peace of nothing
saved, the half-stones smouldering,
the pines no longer dying
but standing in their towers of ash.

I come to the ladder dismantled
and the path of an absent man.
He is drifting through a floor hatch
to his simple tools in the sky: windows,
fire finder, radio phone, his hawk eyes boring
into the horizon as they have for many summers,
his tower anchored by the pilings eighty feet below,
lichen slowing them
to stone now. Firestone,
birthstone, gravestone,
cornerstone,

　　　　　　Oct. 10, 1961, everything younger
then, days until Thanksgiving, the forest
just beginning to die thirty years before
the infra-red scanners retire him. In the home
in Medicine Hat he'd give anything for smoke.
He dreams of ladders and fears the opposite
of heights, his body underground, eyes sealed
by the earth that was always distant.

At the end of the season of fires
the steel crux drones in the wind.
If the men who worked in towers went mad
from solitude and watching, let the mad who walk
                                    through hills
lie down. I am buckbrush in the middle of four stones.
I am rough with remembering,
half shrub, half story
far below the belly of a room in the sky.

Let the tower keep the towerman
and the weary chlorophylls. Let it wait
for the fire that twists the cross braces
and shatters the cupola like a cone.

Let it keep the final fire, the great seas
burning, the towers falling through the world
toward the next one. Let the world no longer die
but fly past itself to the white gazing stars.

A Letter for Newlove

You probably don't remember me. We met
when I was twenty-two on an ugly couch
in a roomful of people in Regina in November,
people talking about your words and the end
of birds. I'd like to live a slower life too,
I think I said. You were an awkward comrade
referring to yourself in the third person, your demons
rustling in the scotch-guarded flowers,
in your snow-haired wing, your open ear.

Where your prairie climbs the Cypress Hills
the flickers hunt in little armies and the living
finally talk to the dead. I am talking, talking,
sorrow in the soft grey chests of the armies,
their brother's wing breaking by a ranchyard
somewhere, a flicker in the dust from the school bus
on the first day of school, the children wiser
than they'll ever be, the coral-red crescent
leaving the nape of the year. A girl gets off
the bus and wants to save him when he needs
a club to smash him into the afterlife
and the summer I was twelve I found
a knocked-out pigeon under the railroad bridge,
made him live in a cage until he loved me. I don't
know how to be unless it gets me something.
The flicker knows the only perfect word,
a war cry, and it leaves a grave more beautiful
than any of your poems, not by much,
just a bit, dear John: I'm leaving
the world. Is there anything you need

up there? I'll bring it the last time I leave here,
the long trucks carrying the cattle to slaughter
and the school bus going home.

One Story

Once,
a girl became a buffalo, a bearded head walking west on the
leg of its tongue until she slept, a brown stone lit by the
grasses, the paths toward her visible from space, a door in
her skin drumming open, thunder, a ticking. The buffalo girl
hollowed, and the cave between her braids watched the ice
seas part around her, the offerings going by, one by one, very
slowly, the ferns and the last of the mastodons and the great
extinct flowers. When the world unfroze it beat with the new,
last buffalo who rubbed their licey sides against her patience,
moon skin to stone, the fluted points landing in the flesh of
the moon herds. She will always be a buffalo, a sleeping clock
above the tired plains, her eye at Head of the Mountain, her
tail at Chimney Coulee where the hides of the last ones peeled
away like the skins of the earth, the last men scratching their
fears on the skin of the earth. This is the short story. The long
one lives in the arrows still arriving, in the ice halfway to the
fires in her tongue.

Not Speaking for One Week

Wind is Pine for *listen*.
Snap means *wait*.
And the shadow word
dangles from the witch's hair
and fights the old war of deadfall and pours
from the one-toothed gargoyles in the eaves of the forest,

in the gardens of the giants, their woody flowers creaking,
the word leaning west, west, growing vertical
against the wind's disorder, the raven trees planted
by one wingtip and flying.

And the word descends the crosses, branch
by feather by root into the land below the cow paths
through the forest of the grass, into the sea
below the cow paths through the forest of the word,

the word is not arriving, the word is here
and blooming and I carry my mouth
on my shoulders, the only branch
I wear when I crash down.

ROOT

Blue Gramma

Priestess of the grasses.
Crescent flower: quarter moon,
mouse's comb, fetus
of the blue bear
hanging. In the dusk
the autumn Blackfoot count.
When the blue gramma grass
has only one flower it will be
a mild winter. Does it mean
the sow will bear single children,
loners, hermits, onlybears, their tracks
and their mothers to talk to?

Fear of Machines

for Hal Gates and IHC

High above the software the autumn is turning toward winter
on its engines of generosity and frost. A blue truck older than its
driver crosses two afternoons to get here, grille smiling forward,
Silver Diamond heart pumping southwest through the harvests.
You block the wheels in the turning hills, home spot, machine
within a machine, sky eager as 1952, Old Reliable hauling in the
seasons on its cloud wheels, sweet October giving out its oranges
to walking. Summer of the blue light, winter of the moonlight,
camper sleeps until you leave, you are the only human between
here and Reesor Lake, the only broken machine, your rattling
body weeping. Someone you love is going to die soon, maybe
you, and the autumn will die of the illness of darkness, the sky
all wheels, and the blue machine in nightmare does not take you
home, a truck cold as its driver, your hand full of ice and too
little throttle on the moonlit backward roll downhill. Fear a
thing enough and it will happen, breakdown, winter here alone,
no books but the *International L130 Owner's and Driver's
Manual* and no tools, a ride toward spring in a blue hearse
pulled by the sky.

The twelfth valve of your heart is burning. Leaves can tell by
listening. They are filling the heat of your wheeling path with
their sound of promised snow and crushing bones. High above
the fear of what has never broken, the poplars are left with their
skins, cylinders of frost giving them and giving them their
motion sleep. An engine waits to take you back. You will be the
only one to leave.

Cattle

Ships of the brome.
The floating dead.
Corpses of the black stars,
Angus faces twinkling in the lodgepoles,
now you see them, now you don't. These
are the cattle of the flat plateau, up here,
everything ghost: the forest rising from decay,
the tiger pacing his sabred absence, the grasses,
ghosts of fire smouldering downward

the cattle whose glass eyes see in black and green,
who carry horns like headdresses, heavy
and ornate, the cattle swaying toward the lip
of the valley when lightning trapped
the grassy sea at the entrance to the night

and their cowboy,
the first cowboy, the cowboy
of the dusk with his grey bandana
wanders with them, his eyeless horse
rounding up the dead, their horns
piercing air, the moons
of their stomachs orbiting the trees.

Prayer

A wild girl's footprints have fallen
through the winters, earth stars
light up the air. There have been no bears
in the Cypress Hills for a hundred and twenty years
but I follow the Ursa below me, Aiekunekwe
in the undertrees, rippling sand of her fur,
coulees breaking in the deep hearts
of the chokecherries. She
is the muscled cloud turning logs
to look for slugs, shit fossils blooming
with tannin in the black sky made of the dead.
In her skull the root of the bullet
has grown its tree of stars and in the creek
the trout are swimming around the hole
in water where Isaac Cowie dipped his cup
and counted to seven hundred fifty.

There have been no bears in the Grizzly Hills
since before the great fire, since the last bear
dropped into 1885 like a mountain falls
into the ocean, all the thunders sinking.
There have been no bears for three
of my unfinished lives, my night lives.
She climbs from the ground and pads
around my canvas. She is sad
and skinny. I talk with my smell.
From the hollow just outside of me
your claws light up the trees.

The Meadow, Fear of Cattle

On the other side of the golden bean at the end
of Meiers Road, a cow and yearling steer, Red Angus
crosses, the blackfly music of their cud. A skull
spreads its horns to the flowers, fall to the coyotes,
old head thinking in its white house under the trees.
If the cattle are mourning then grief is peace,
a soft belch from the rumen, the molars
sending fescue to its next three lives where the cattle
have become the wild animals, cinnamon bears dreaming
of their winters in the barns of the earth, never knowing
the demon bird, a crow crossed with a harrier,
a grey Ominous, a cross.

                        How afraid I have been
of cattle, of their size in a china room, their steaming
necks and boiling stomachs, hooves branding the earth,
their boulder heads lowered, horns like the fangs of gods.
Young Red stretches from his post-cud sleep, bearbull hungry
as spring. He is walking toward me, igniting the flowers,
he is reading my nervous poisons, the meadow hot
and blinding as the ring in Las Ventas. I spread
my arms to his hot green roar, now his tongue
around my hand, the rasp tongue the rancher's wife
would have carried to the house in a chipped enamel bowl
at slaughtering time in the old days, the grey fish
tossing on the cutting board, saying haiku, saying
you have to be strong to work with cattle,
saying *you've had a hard life, hasn't everyone?*
Red throws his horns. I clap my hands, gunshot:
he follows his mother to the next huge green fescue plate.

Haiku for Texas Gates

The fences are eating
the animals. An opening—
the ground eats my hooves.

The Hound and the Owlets
in the silence of Uisge Beatha

Blodeuwedd in half-sleep
talks through wool, her Flower Face
in the snow wool, the mice
asleep in their bunkers

She was the owl who rode my mother's back
when I was small as an owlet, harmless
and closed-eyed, hound in a nest

She was the owl in the deer
I called Blodeuwedd, Flower Face
in the lodgepoles, the deer
I answered with the chase

She was the owl with the two woolly daughters
waiting for their feathers when I ran down
from the mountain and came upon their backs
The four moons turned
The owlets flapped from my giant
mouth into the bouncing branches
and there appeared the owl, a flying bull,
in her talons, my brindle head

Insomnia, Battle Creek Valley

I am beginning to believe I will never sleep
again. I am sold to the creatures
of the wakeful night, my black cell
dividing and dividing into more alertnesses,
regret twisting inward, sleeping bag
tangled in my hope. Here in the woods
at night are the people I must apologize
to, faces rising in the blood inside
my eyelids while the guiltless worlds
outside of me lie awake in unison.

Eleven nights I've lain awake. I will not
fall into the night for even one hour, body
trembling at the cliffs of sleep, rock body refusing
to be sand, mule body pulling backward,
steel body, rebar bone, black blood clanking
in the block walls of my brain, canvas against
the centre pole, morning at the red need for sleep.

Seven hours ago I lay down facing
west, sunfall, windrise, brace against
the valley's taking. Above me
is the feathered question I am too tired
to answer. My ear is the answer, and the night
ticking. There are beats between the owl's calls,
twenty-five of them. There is a bone
in the dark, rusting.
There are white nerves dying
below my counting skin.

Blue Gramma

Crescent flower: question on its side, asking
where I come from. I say from my blue mother,

from my grandma before, the one who would have
died by cold on a field below the stars, the one

who floats inside of me, grasses in her hands
in the womb below the ocean, my cave

below the ocean. She is on her way
to her wedding, her winter wedding.

She is travelling down a tunnel of snow
and beginning to swim away.

West Benson Trail, The Ford, Fear of Water

The road is its own bridge under knee-deep water.
I roll up my pants to walk barefoot through the burning
cold, the green speeding night, I could slip on the rocks and be swept
into the train water, the liquid wind. I am afraid of being born into
the wisdom of the sailors no longer thrashing, afraid
like the drowned boy's mother who sank to the bottom
of her tears, the girl thrown from the dock when the narrow ones
knew she couldn't swim, the bee-fish
poisoning her nostrils.

                The clover road on the other side
waits for my foot to step forward. It is winter again, I'm walking
the edge of the Frenchman, a jaw swallowing my leg
to the knee. The black stone had been following below
the ice, and the lodgepoles leave holes in the earth
when the wind throws them down, the stones between
their roots like fish eggs at the openings to the sea,
its scaly bodies leaping for air. I have met their weedy eyes
and looked away, the vision line a liquid bridge, the only
bridge there is, the living entering the waters.

Wish

You have no right to be here, must be here
lightly, make your body small. Tiptoe

through the poplars and the leaves shatter
slowly, almost fooled into thinking you want

nothing from them. You want them
to stay autumn, whole and falling, to let you

belong and not be seen. But first lay down
your hurtling tools and language on the path

of the coyote descended from the coyote
who never heard gunshot. Take care of his deaths,

of the speed your crashing gives his feet, of the distance
from you where pulse cools, sundown, crimson in his voice,

cousins answering the dusk. Take care of his joy,
of your wanting. Almost die every day and live. You must take

care to take nothing: underlit clouds belong to the end
of words, leaves give themselves to the act

of the walk. Take care of their pieces like mirrors,
count the faces of your families, let night

erase your tracks.

Battle Creek Road

is the road I haven't walked yet,

here, where it will happen again. History
                    repeats itself and the road that follows the creek
crosses it twice, timber bridges over deep green water
                        feeding the root of the hills and the starving

path to the shrine of the bison, end of the longest
                    winter. What is left to say about the massacre?
The dark white spruce gather in their walls,
                  fortresses of grandmothers. Above the road

to Fort Walsh three weeks before the solstice
                is a rose road, tea apple. In the centre of one rose
is a bee who burrowed to the centre of a head
                    tied to a lodgepole, the metal eagle flying

from the Winchester to Akitchita's heart. No one
                  knows what really happened but the owls
who were wakened by the shots and the maiden owls
                  screaming. What is left to say is the reason

I don't sleep here. The dead breathe in the wind
                    and in the gas from the chambers
and in the jungles growing from the dust of the Mayan
                  temples, the last exhalations raging:

Lost River.

Creek

Green water, tree mirror, the steadfast white spruce stare
could save all of us: deep creek in the deeper valley,
the churning, fevered, great-horned creek
in the mosquito and Canada violet valley, the jungle
bulging with rain, horsetail knowing like cow parsnip
that the end of rain is drought and the creek,

an asylum of water, would take us
swirling only just downward, its artery carve
through gravity knowing all along where it is
going, slow creek pulling the water tons
past me, shallows quickly, quickly

washing stones and when I wash, naked
from the waist, sweat and sebum flowing
eastward, the creek delivers me, cold
and not yet flawed, potatoes boil

in its water, the eaten creek inside me
and the vessel I take from here falls
in the first town, water running

away from me, my only water,
water that will not be water

in any other world.

Battle Creek Hill, Fear of Death

I am not afraid of dying but of being
left behind, my father and mother, my hound
and my lover, my friends and my rivers
leaving me
in this fearful coat in the winter
of the next forty years,
my fingers freezing in the starry fields
as my cerebellum dreams its tiny nightmares,
my body running like a spooked horse to the cliffs
where the stars' teeth fall away and the earth
sends forth its waterfalls of blood.

Eyes fall from the poplars, snow eyes.
In the naked trees my eye in the mountain
watches the road, dust river leading
from the hospices, the dead limping by
in their rags, blind and arriving. On the wind
is my father four hundred miles away, his body struck
like a clock's chime, thumping onto the groceries,
breaking the eggs, his body born German in 1924,
crashing to the humus of the soldiers, his rib cage
in his arms like his perfect only born.

Alone among the dead I have arrived.
I will leave here blank and invisible, a mirror
signalling to the good and steady star of the cold.
It will feel like the Monday morning after the war
when everything emptied and was, it will feel
like the end of the world.

Inside Tower Road

The hottest of ten hot evenings: the sun
refuses to fall and water has never weighed more.
Tonight I will sleep at the top of Tower Road.
Water will ride me there, being here is cowboy,
I am the horse, an obstinate buckskin plodding
the dry hill out of the valley, a jug
on both flanks: rock water, lead water,
rocking water leading.

           Air is a horse
sweating under June's fast weight, air is wet
with the promise of thunder, air will carry
no more light,

           grass is a horse,
a green running light,

           flowers are the light's
tears splitting open,

           and the horse of light reaches
the inside of the year and turns
above its journey.

Wide hill lodgepole
arthritic over its flowerbed, its music
for the flowers. Wisdom twists
toward the clocks:
field chickweed, small face,
ten petals in the year, ten
half-seasons. The longest
is this road again, ruts full
of brome, clear-cuts ticking
with thistles, teenaged lodgepoles
crowding against the sunset. I will climb
this road again in the gold half
of the year's second summer, the honey leaves
raining. I will remember this singing dusk,

heat tricks, a guy-wire whistle
refracted by the cooling wind to the sound
of a distant chainsaw, my thousand steps
listening before looking up. Above the trees,
an orange head. The aisle between old tire tracks
leads to the priest at the start of fires, I am marrying
myself, circling the cupola from the ground,
the future hovering.

Pumpkin Face.

Devil Face.

Blanket Flower.

Evening Star.

My stations of arrival in the year's
shortest night, in the blessed, breathing
land of the night trees. I place
the flowers of my reaching.
The waters funnel through me.

Fallen

In the light from knives
I will not fight. The stone has split,
cut my hand, left its bloodline, warrior mark
on the hillface, red streak drying as truth. Stone
is fallen where it cut me with truth, my body
running to water, the Battle Creek healing its banks
of blood and rot-gut whisky for a hundred years
and more with water from the mountains that will not
make me more thirsty, the red pasts swirling
in the water turning clear.

I am empty and no longer noise.
The morning after stone my cloth hand is
a banner unravelling. I hold it up, surrender:
now that I can love I must begin.

WINDLIGHT

Night Tree

Dusk in the narrow country
of the North Plateau. The lodgepoles have been
waiting, villages of the undead with their arms
out, the night clerks of stone hotels
with broken beds and caving basements.

I enter, cambium locking,
and the father of doors knows
I will wake without a body. *Choose your tree.*

In a country disappearing over cliffs, invisible
bones in the bone trees, mine is the lodgepole
of the hot pasture's edge, candelabra
in the Church of Pine, a year's hymns
bundled in the flames that light my death.

A low branch opens: back room, needle dust,
hip hollow last lain in before the discovery
of magnetic north. The hound who has been following
circles its sleep and lays down a long bone line.
It has followed for years toward this bearing,
muzzle pointing through the tree
to the north northwest of the afterlight.

I lie down also, kiss the velvet bone, hound skull
spearing its heartbeat, my arm around the great chest
thumping slowly and more slowly,
for a seasons-long minute
not at all. I am alone among
the dead again, a spoon
around the dark spoon of the hound
who will hover in the branches,
someone staring north
from Lodgepole, Montana,
the Hound Star rising.

I will live alone if I must, leave
for the coyotes the gift of flesh and lung,
I will walk downhill abandoned
in the flickering morning.

Strobe lights flash over lake beds
nights of walking to the west,
the tree bucking in the lightning wind,
a cold wave, a warm wave, storms
seconds long, no rain, the fear of thunder
curled against my fear of pine. Lodgepoles crash
within earshot, too dark to run, the hound awake
and trembling in the tossing night, coyotes dreaming
of our crushed flesh below the toppled dark,
the star erased by daylight.

Through a tunnel in the branches a half moon,
company, an eye. Between winds the pine
holds its stare. I believe in the top of storm,
in luck, nothing safer, in the beating
under the rocking tree.

4,567 Feet

Someone said we start climbing when we reach
the mountain top. Stones say we must not
seek. Stones ran from the man with the altimeter,
Cailletet's rider searching on this flat plateau
for the Cypress furthest from the seas.

The numbers followed one another
like seasons or cattle and stones
ran home to pray for him.

The road has lost its body, sent me
forth beyond South Benson Trail.
This is the prairie with its hand
over the wars, the sinless bluegrass
Carry the Kettle prairie after prairie where the souls
of cattle wander after slaughter, amnesty deep
in the lodgepoles above the deserted world.

Cartographer, mathematician, I come
into the elevation winds to find
the measured place, the magnet for stone, the drum
stars spiral out of, sun brothers pulsing in their names.
On the dizzy frontal bone of the hills no bells
wait, no stake periscopes from the depths of grass
but the bright stone will announce itself,
I will see to the mouth of the river
a hundred valleys away and the souls
will answer from the trees.

I want perfect words.
I'll take the excellence of altitude.

I seek, I seek, the prophet
who'll return from the shining
edge of infinity

but the shining
floats away. Lost River
rises from the auricles, the grasses howling
who do you think you are, blonde fangs
in the eye, elk crashing up, my sight in pieces.
All along the hills have been laughing and now
in the dusk north is freezing
where the west should be,
there is no bright stone
and I'll sleep in the cold
to prove otherwise.

Pine bough, willow bough.
I gather my bed.

A stream of white
stones, a crease in the trees.
Cutline! Saviour!

Everest wasn't Everest until they wanted
it climbed, it was just a happy mountain.
I am running through forests on the path
between the mapped land and the lost one,
stumbling down from the non-point to the mouth
of roads, the truck and its heater a mile north
by windlight. Polaris is leaping on the highest
point in the prairie. The nameless measure goes
about its evening and the shamans become the star.

Forty-One Stones

With this ring the fathers
marry the mountains, the choir
of the wounded forgets the start of the song,
singing *this is the world and was always
the world.* The wheel invents me. I must step
away, dig a hole in the grass with a stick,
a black mouth singing my vanishing.
I breathe earth like a stone breathes.
I breathe the grave of my bed.

The wheel turns, stone-go-round,
it writhes, a wreathe of worms
around the choosing: that stone
for its question, that stone for its wolf back,
that stone for its eye in the shoulder, the stones
two men rolled, four men, the stone placed
by the boy going blind from answers.
From my hiding I ask *May I ride the stone
with the grey and green saddle of lichen?*
and the eyes close, more open than before.

I ride from here to the sun.
I ride to the dark beginning.
I ride to the seeds at the core of the earth.
I ride to my last life.

The wheel turns above the door to the earth,
the eye in the empty pouch of my clothes.

The Last Tower Road

I am waiting for the last night. The cattle
bed down in the trees. A ranch light twinkles
forty miles to the north in the breathing grasses.
This is not night
but smoke from the bright lands
cooling, horizon smouldering
with the rhizome of the sun, not night
but shadow's ancestors climbing from the paint
of fire and shedding the light of their skin.

Hilltops are the ends of hills, solstice
the end of summer. The slow dark
floats in the forests already weary
with work, they have been building roads
toward the sky, they have been climbing
to the temple and do not always believe.

The angel who stopped waiting
can speak now. He throws his cones
from my lodgepole tree. The dawn
will swoop across my last path,
my owl, my cowboy, my love.

Initiation

Warm wind sleepwalks to the late November hills,
a summer from the mountains, the only snow
in white lines the shadow-widths of trees.
My body that was dying
climbs into the chance of the birdless hills, here
in the late hills nothing sings but light singing
summer and its duty of darkness, sweet
contradiction, a humid dream, a lost day
from the future or the disappointed past. The future
will remember the high snow rising at the forest edge,
prairie wool reaching for August more
than it knows, a lodgepole piling
antlers at its feet and hearing lightning.

What the hills still need to tell me
they will tell me in the air gone mountain, possible,
granite in its smell. Along the precipice of the last month
of the year, a dandelion at the centre of its frozen leaves,
a star no longer leading to the forest
but its gates. The shadow of this lost day
is pine beyond contorta at the border
of the constant wind, the hunchbacked lodgepole,
the pot-bellied lodgepole, the joker braiding
with the leaner and the kneeler.

In the gallery of the damned
I belong. One of the fallen rolls
into a ball of light and drags me
back to the day. How my adrenaline calls
me worthless, how the clown pines call me

worthless, how my cold breath calls me flawed
by wanting, good for no loveliness
and here to forget, to empty my weight
on the muscled hills beginning to lurch
below me, user, user, dropping oil cans
of fear, plastic loneliness pails,
my empty, heavy, rusting skin.

And still the fallen ghost who once was worthless
calls me humble, last offer in the winter light,
my blood washing through
to the slow drip of silence. I will not enter
the forest. I have crossed it, fallen through
myself, finally hollowed, the beetles
moving in to scour me out.

A Letter for Stegner

I have used up my provisions.
At the end of the rolling east, in the house
built by your father the bootlegger
I begin again. Wallace, what did you dream
in the shadow of the west when you wished
you were alone? Did your mother
hear you dreaming?

I have come to my last supper,
the silver meal of the berry, bright
silver, and the candy of its stone.

Did you ever suck on the wolf willow seed
to keep from feeling thirsty? It's a petrified tear,
you know, a drop, a top, a toy earth, and longitudes
are deer paths older than anything.
I have found the last weeping. Spit
is my water. The storm in my mouth
has an eye. No salt rises
in the found tooth on your tongue.

Windlight

Below the emerald star the wind reveals
the cure. The highest point above the sea

is the road through the sea. My cloak is my sail.
My skull parts the air. I leave the edge of the earth

for the second earth, the sea above the earth.
I sail to the day at the core of hills, the people

who have gone there have not returned. The wind
lands where my eye was, a cone in its talons.

It has flown from the mouth of the Road
of Giving Up. It leaves one seed in my dust.

Endward

Equinox burns in the poplars along the road to the fire tower on the Saskatchewan side of the West Block of the Cypress Hills, the road of many roads on a day of many days, the road where everything will end. The tower is dismantled by the only people I have ever seen here, the cupola crashing down one windowed leaf at a time, one for each half-direction. My second landmark leaves me. The first was the leaning barn at the edge of Leask that told me we were halfway north and left me without measures like the end of summer does. Now the pines are watched from space. Nothing rises from the distance to say where I am, the slopes blonde and humanless as they were for the Plano. I go back to Cypress, I go back, rain or winter smouldering. I have the shapes of hills, every bone with its curve, the backs of ancient horses. The forest and the dead holding it to the sun.

Highway 271 North

You come out of the hills,
out of hiding, out of the canvas nightroom, circus tent
of the mad, the ghosts came swinging at you
on trapezes of falling stars and you did not sleep
and you did not sleep. Deer leapt through
their shining hoops of grief and gazed
into your soundlessness, sleeplessness
more silent than sleep, the roar of dream
below your ghosts, mouth denying
your songs of blood, ears and the hollows
of your eyes bleeding quietly at the night, hearing
and seeing nothing. And the ghosts in their costumes
of frost on their meteor ropes leapt out to you,
blinding arcs across your tent roof, they landed
in the darkness of your open arms, they glowed
with space and stayed with you. Go now from the hills
toward sleep, you are no longer hiding. The night
flashes out, the cold in your body falls away,
the hills bleed into your leaving.

Cargo

In the last white month the centuries begin
to breathe less slowly. Groggy animals are waking,
the hulls of the pine ships half-sunk in snow, the living
holding out the world in their green feathered hands,
its punctured hearts turning.

I have been sad among lodgepoles.
The winds on their spines are the oceans
washing up the dead, the winds are distant
cavalries, they are coming for me, the winds
ask the forest deep inside the moon,
the unmapped moon still burning.

On my bear's feet I walk through
the churches. I drag a great sled.
It is piled with the bodies.
I wrap them in the pieces of my skin,
I hang them in the branches.

NOTES

Forward
cyprès: There are no cypress trees in the Cypress Hills. The predominant species at the higher elevations is the lodgepole pine. *Cyprès* is Métis French for jack pine or lodgepole pine; it is standard French for cypress. When the Métis named the hills *les montagnes des cyprès,* they were calling them, literally, the Pine Mountains. As Americans and Euro-Canadians moved into the area, the name was assumed to be standard French and was translated as such. "The Cypress Hills" is a misnomer.

Tower Road
DNR: Department of Natural Resources, a former incarnation of a Saskatchewan government department.

Prayer
Isaac Cowie: a Hudson's Bay Company trader of furs and hides.

The Hound and the Owlets
Blodeuwedd: the Celtic owl goddess.

Battle Creek Road
the massacre: On June 1, 1873, twenty Assiniboine were killed in a battle with American wolfers near the future site of Fort Walsh, the first North West Mounted Police headquarters.

4,567 Feet
Cailletet: Louis Paul Cailletet was the French physicist who invented the altimeter.

Endward
the Plano: big game hunters thought to have lived throughout the plains from 8,000 to 4,000 B.C.

ACKNOWLEDGEMENTS

Earlier versions of some of these poems appeared in *Event*, *The Fiddlehead*, *Grain*, *The Malahat Review*, and *Open Wide a Wilderness: Canadian Nature Poems*, and were broadcast on CBC Radio. "Fear of Machines" was a winner in the prose poem category of the 2004 Short *Grain* Contest. Several of these poems also appeared as a chapbook, *Tower Road*, published by JackPine Press in December 2004.

I am grateful to the Saskatchewan Arts Board for the generosity that allowed me to focus on this book, and to the Saskatchewan Writers/Artists Colonies for treasured retreat time. Thanks to the Eastend Arts Council for several wondrous stays in the Wallace Stegner House, and to Sharon Butala for her vision in establishing it as a refuge for writers.

Deepest thanks to Travis Carey, Tim Lilburn, Dave Margoshes, Elizabeth Philips, Seán Virgo, and Paul Wilson for their wisdom and insight during various stages of the manuscript's development. Gratitude to Don McKay for his patience as an editor, his faith in my landscape, and for helping me get lost to find my way.

"Ranger Station Road" is for Kevin Redden.
"Work Road, North Benson Trail" is for the Cypress crew of June 1993.
"One Story" is for Trevor Herriot.
"Forty-One Stones" is for Don Domanski.

Thanks, as always, to Hal, who has been there since the first Cypress.

A bow to the loyal grace of Uisge Beatha: she was bred to sprint but walked with me to the ends of the earth.

Barbara Klar's previous books are *The Night You Called Me a Shadow* (co-winner of the 1993 Gerald Lampert Award) and *The Blue Field*, both from Coteau Books. She has worked as a tree planter, camp cook, editor, mentor, and freelance writer for both print and radio. She lives in an old farmhouse northwest of Saskatoon.